# The Khwan Niamut

THE IOWA
SZATHMÁRY
CULINARY ARTS SERIES

Edited by David E. Schoonover

# *The Khwan Niamut*

*Edited by David E. Schoonover*

University of Iowa Press   Iowa City

# or, Nawab's Domestic Cookery

University of Iowa Press, Iowa City 52242

Copyright © 1992 by the University of Iowa Press

All rights reserved

Printed in the United States of America

Design by Richard Hendel

96   95   94   93   92   C   5   4   3   2   1

Library of Congress Cataloging-in-Publication Data

The Khwan Niamut; or, Nawab's domestic cookery/edited by
    David E. Schoonover.

    p.      cm.—(The Iowa Szathmáry culinary arts series)

    Includes bibliographical references.

    ISBN 0-87745-394-2 (acid-free paper)

    1. Cookery, Iranian.    2. Cookery—Iran—

History.    3. Home economics—Iran—History.

I. Schoonover, David E.    II. Title: Nawab's

domestic cookery.    III. Series.

TX723.I7K48    1993

641.5955—dc20                    92-30763                CIP

Illustrations reproduced from Joannes de Laet's *PERSIA seu
REGNI PERSICI Status*. Lugd. Batav. [Leyden]: Ex Officina
Elzeveriana, 1633, through the courtesy of the Special Collec-
tions Department, the University of Iowa Libraries, Iowa City.

# Contents

# Foreword

## David E. Schoonover

### THE PERSIAN PAST

*The Khwan Niamut; or, Nawab's Domestic Cookery* is a small book from an intriguing time in Anglo-Persian history. Now published in facsimile from the edition printed in Calcutta in 1839, this book embodies a curious concoction of languages, locales, cultures, and cuisines. An anonymous translator prepared the text, drawing upon a "small Pamphlet, in the Persian Language. . . ." It was published in Calcutta rather than Persia, avowedly for the "European Community" but presumably for the "Inglis-ha," as the English would have been called in Farsi, the Persian language. It reflects an extraordinary mixture of European involvement in the Middle East—a state of affairs often described as "The Great Game"—that was played out through much of the nineteenth century in Persia, India, and Afghanistan.

1

In *The Persians amongst the English: Episodes in Anglo-Persian History*, Denis Wright provides a helpful summary of Anglo-Persian relationships which may account for some of *The Khwan Niamut*'s peculiarities:

Until the English established themselves in India they had no regular contact with the Persians. The East India Company, founded by royal charter in 1600, was the early channel through which Anglo-Persian relations developed. The Company shipped a first consignment of English woolens to Persia in 1616. . . . afterwards they opened trading posts, manned by Company officials from home, in a number of southern Persian towns. . . . It was not until 1807 that the British Government considered relations with Persia of sufficient importance to justify the appointment of Sir Harford Jones as their first resident envoy at the Persian capital in Tehran. . . . The decision by London to send out Harford Jones to represent them at the Qajar Court had been stimulated by growing fears that the French planned to attack India through Persia. Jones' task was to secure their expulsion from Persia and to re-

place the 1807 Franco-Persian Treaty of
Finkenstein with an Anglo-Persian Treaty
of Friendship and Alliance. (Pp. xiv–xv)

Wright notes some circumstances that may
be relevant to *The Khwan Niamut* being published in Calcutta rather than in Persia:

Twice during the nineteenth century—in
1838 and again in 1856—diplomatic relations between England and Persia were
broken off. On both occasions the British
not only withdrew their Missions from
Tehran but also occupied Kharg Island in
the Persian Gulf as a means of bringing
pressure on the Persian Government. . . .

In both 1838 and 1856 British opposition
to Persian aspirations to regain posses-
sion of the ancient city of Herat, then in
Afghan hands, lay at the centre of the
quarrel. . . . In 1838 there were troubles
over the arrest of a Persian messenger
[one Ali Reza Beg, who was seized and
stripped by the Persian army]; alleged in-
sults to the British Resident in Bushire
and a dispute over housing in Tehran. . . .
(P. 102)

*The Khwan Niamut* reveals an aristocratic
household's "domestic cookery" that is inter-

3

national in interest, translating a particular nawab's luxurious recipes from Persian into English, thereby providing "the best HIN-DOOSTNEE DISHES to the European Community. . . ." In addition, this book's appendix reveals a pronounced English bias for Boiled Calf's Head, Collared Eels, Eel Pie, and Hashed Mutton. If these dishes reflect a British hegemony as well as the colonial's homesickness, the rest of the book's "most Flavoured and Savoury Dishes, from the kitchen of Nawab Qasim Uli Khan, Bujadur Qâum Jung," are examples of an elevated style of Persian cuisine, prepared in generous proportions. The first two recipes, for Ukhnee Poolao and Plain Poolao, call for "Kid, one."

For many contemporary readers, James Morier had described just such a marvelous feast in one of the most popular novels of the century, *The Adventures of Hajji Baba of Ispahan*, first published in London in 1824, with other editions following in 1828, 1835, 1856, 1863, 1897, and well into the twentieth century. In chapter 24—"A Description of the Entertainment"—Morier tantalized his readers by letting them gaze surreptitiously as the shah dined:

The only persons, besides servants, admitted into the saloon where the Shah dined, were the three princes, his sons, who had accompanied him; and they stood at the farthest end, with their backs against the wall, attired in dresses of ceremony, with swords by their sides. Mirza Ahmak remained in attendance without. A cloth, of the finest Cashmerian shawl fringed with gold, was then spread on the carpet before the king by the chief of the valets, and a gold ewer and basin were presented for washing hands. The dinner was then brought in trays, which, as a precaution against poison, had been sealed with the signet of the head steward before they left the kitchen, and were broken open by him again in the presence of the Shah. Here were displayed all the refinements of cookery. Rice, in various shapes, smoked upon the board; first, the *chilau*, as white as snow; then the *pilau*, with a piece of boiled lamb smothered in the rice; then another *pilau*, with a baked fowl in it; a fourth, coloured with saffron, mixed up with dried peas; and, at length, the king of Persian dishes, the *narinj pillau*, made with slips

5

of orange-peel, spices of all sorts, almonds, and sugar; salmon and herring, from the Caspian Sea, were seen among the dishes, and trout from the river Zengi, near Erivan; then, in china basins and bowls of different sizes, were the ragouts, which consisted of hash made of a fowl boiled to rags, stewed up with rice, sweet herbs, and onions; a stew, in which was a lamb's marrow-bone, with some loose flesh about it, and boiled in its own juice; small gourds, crammed with force-meat, and done in butter; a fowl stewed to rags, with a brown sauce of prunes; a large omelette, about two inches thick; a cup full of the essence of meat, mixed up with rags of lamb, almonds, prunes, and tamarinds, which was poured upon the top of the *chilau*; a plate of poached eggs, fried in sugar and butter; a dish of *badenjans*, slit in the middle and boiled in grease; a stew of venison, and a great variety of other messes too numerous to mention. After these came the roasts. A lamb was served up hot from the spit, the tail of which, like marrow, was curled up over its back. Partridges, and, what is looked upon as the rarest delicacy in

Persia, two *capk dereh*, partridges of the valley, were procured on the occasion. Pheasants from Mazanderan were there also, as well as some of the choicest bits of the wild ass and antelope. The display and the abundance of delicacies surprised every one; and they were piled up in such profusion around the king, that he seemed almost to form a part of the heap. I do not mention the innumerable little accessories of preserves, pickles, cheese, butter, onions, celery, salt, pepper, sweets, and sours, which were to be found in different parts of the tray, for that would be tedious; but the sherbets were worthy of notice, from their peculiar delicacy: these were contained in immense bowls of the most costly china, and drank by the help of spoons of the most exquisite workmanship, made of the pear tree. They consisted of the common lemonade, made with superior art; of the *sekenjebin*, or vinegar, sugar, and water, so mixed that the sour and sweet were as equally balanced as the blessings and miseries of life; the sherbet of sugar and water, with rose-water to give it a perfume, and sweet seeds to increase

its flavour; and that made of the pomegranate; all highly cooled by lumps of
floating ice.

The king, then, doubling himself down
with his head reclining towards his food,
buried his hand in the pilaus and other
dishes before him, and ate in silence,
whilst the princes and the servants-in-
waiting, in attitudes of respect, remained
immovable. When he had finished he got
up, and walked into an adjoining room,
where he washed his hands, drank his coffee, and smoked his *kalian* or water-pipe.
(Pp. 193–195)

## THE RECENT PRESENT

During the final years of the reign of the last
shah of shahs over the Persian Empire, feasts
such as the one just described would still be
served. On tables covered with *qalamkar*, the
block-printed floral cloth, would appear hand-
hammered trays mounded with the same *narinj pilau*, seasoned with fresh sweet Persian oranges. Other trays of silver, brass,
and copper held the lambs—roasted, broiled,

stewed—surrounded by saffron rice. The usual accompaniments were fresh cucumber, mint, dill, and cilantro salads, yogurt dressings, pickles and relishes, platters of thin baked breads called *nan* or *barbaree*, and pitchers of fruit *sharbat*.

My wife, Jane, and I learned to appreciate the beauties of Persian arts and cuisines during the two years that we lived in Iran, from the summer of 1975 through late spring of 1977. I was just completing my Ph.D. in English language and literature at Princeton University when an announcement arrived advertising teaching positions at Jundi Shapur University in Ahwaz, Iran. The university offered two-year contracts with paid round-trip transportation and tempted us by describing archaeological sites, an eighteen-hole all-sand golf course, and exotic foods.

When we arrived in Ahwaz, the capital of the oil-producing province of Khuzestan in southwestern Iran, we lived at the Hotel Ahwaz for a month, pending the completion of our faculty apartment. During that month we began to explore Persian cuisine, from the national dish of grilled lamb kabobs to the university chancellor's multicourse formal dinner with whole roast lambs on each banquet table surrounded by soups, salads, mounds of rice, and trays of cookies and pastries. At the hotels and restaurants we sampled most items from the menus—more kabobs from lamb (Kabab-e Barg) and chicken (Kabab-e Joojeh), a feast dish of duckling in pomegranate-walnut sauce (Fesenjan-e Ordak), a breakfast omelette with green herbs (Kookoo-ye Sabzi), *pollos* or rice dishes containing meat or fowl and seasoned with fruit and nuts, chicken with sour cherries (Albaloo Pollo), and rice seasoned with fresh dill, fava beans, and lamb (Baghali Pollo).

As soon as our apartment was ready, we were glad to leave the hotel and start to cook for ourselves. Our first surprise came when we examined the cooking stove, with regular burners on top. When we opened the oven door there sat the butane gas cylinder. Quickly I asked about an oven and was told, "Persians don't use ovens," to which my reply, "But we're not Persians," made no difference. So we realized that much of our cooking would be in skillets, saucepans, and a pressure cooker. Next we bought a small tin charcoal brazier and skewers to cook kabobs, then learned the location deep in the bazaar where the charcoal-man provided real charred-wood fuel, not the familiar briquets.

We shopped for most of our prepared ingredients in Western-style supermarkets and specialty stores, buying imported frozen chickens from many countries of the world, excellent lamb from the meat bazaar, and all fresh vegetables and herbs from the *sabzi* bazaar, or green shop. Of course the most wonderful aromas came from the spice bazaar, where bulk sacks of turmeric, saffron, cumin, dried limes and lemons, ginger, cloves, powdered sumac, almonds, and salted pistachios stood open. The freshest, thickest yogurt came from a corner shop, and across from the university campus we stopped each day to buy just-baked flatbread and usually ate half the batch before getting home.

The following recipes are adapted, with numerous modifications, from Nesta Ramazani's *Persian Cooking: A Table of Exotic Delights.* I have prepared all these dishes either while living in Iran or since returning to the United States. They are typical of the variety of Persian cooking and provide unusual combinations of ingredients and techniques to produce dishes that are truly fit for the nawab's superb dinner table.

## ACKNOWLEDGMENTS

I would like to express my appreciation to Mojgan Seraji for assistance with unfamiliar terms and to these colleagues at the University of Iowa Libraries for their encouragement and assistance with this project: Sheila Creth, Edward Shreeves, Robert McCown, Susan Hansen, and Margaret Richardson.

## REFERENCES

Mary S. Atwood, *A Taste of India*. Boston: Houghton Mifflin, 1969.

*A Handbook for Travellers in India, Burma and Ceylon*. 11th ed., London: John Murray; Calcutta: Thacker, Spink & Co., 1924.

J. J. Morier, *The Adventures of Hajji Baba of Ispahan*. First published by John Murray, London, 1824; edition cited published by Lawrence & Bullen, Ltd., London, 1897.

Nesta Ramazani, *Persian Cooking: A Table of Exotic Delights*. New York: Quadrangle/New York Times Book Co., 1974.

Donald N. Wilber, *Iran Past and Present*. Princeton, N.J.: Princeton University Press, 1975.

Denis Wright, *The Persians amongst the English: Episodes in Anglo-Persian History*. London: I. B. Tauris, 1985.

# Contemporary Persian Recipes

## Appetizers

### YOGURT WITH HERBS (Mast-e Kisei)

Mix plain yogurt with chopped fresh dill weed and/or any of the following: chopped, seeded cucumbers; green seedless grapes; mint and scallions; fresh cilantro; chopped almonds.

Use these cooling combinations as dips with fresh or toasted pita bread.

# Soups

YOGURT SOUP (Ashe-e Mast)

*Serves 6–8*

*1 large onion, chopped*
*2 tablespoons butter or shortening*
*1/2 pound shoulder of lamb or lamb shank or
    ground beef*
*1/4 cup dried chick-peas*
*1/4 cup dried white navy beans*
*1/2 cup dried lentils*
*1 cup rice*
*2 tablespoons salt, or to taste*
*1 teaspoon turmeric*
*1/4 teaspoon pepper*
*3–4 quarts water*
*2–3 cups yogurt*
*1/2 cup chopped fresh parsley as garnish*
*thin slices of lemon as garnish*

Sauté the onion in the butter or shortening
in a large pot until brown. Add the meat and
brown it. Add all the other ingredients except
the yogurt, cover, and simmer for 2 to 3 hours,

or until the chick-peas and beans are done; the lentils should be added after the other ingredients have simmered for 1 hour. Remove the meat from the soup, remove the bone and shred the meat, and return the meat to the soup. Stir a few spoonfuls of hot soup into the yogurt to warm it and prevent curdling; then add the yogurt to the soup, stirring gently. Add chopped parsley and/or very thin slices of lemon as a garnish.

---

## BEAN SOUP WITH MEAT
### (Ashe-e Gooshti)
*Serves 4–6*
*1 large onion, chopped*
*1–2 tablespoons butter or shortening*
*1 bunch fresh parsley, chopped*
*1/2 pound fresh beet greens or spinach, chopped*
*1/4 pound leeks, chopped*
*1/2 pound lamb shank or ground beef*
*1/2 cup dried lentils, presoaked*
*1/4 cup dried navy beans, presoaked*
*1/4 cup dried chick-peas, presoaked*
*1 1/2 teaspoons turmeric*
*1/4 teaspoon pepper*

2 tablespoons salt, or to taste
1 cup rice
2–3 quarts water

Brown the onion in the butter or shortening in a large pot. Add all the other ingredients; the lentils should be added after the other ingredients have simmered for 1 hour. Cover and simmer until the meat is tender (about 1 1/2 to 2 hours). Remove the meat from the soup, bone it, and shred it; return it to the pot.

---

PRUNE SOUP (Ashe-e Aloo)
*Serves 6–8*
1 large onion, chopped
2 tablespoons butter or shortening
4 quarts water
1 cup rice
1 tablespoon turmeric
2 tablespoons salt, or to taste
1/4 teaspoon pepper
1/2 cup dried yellow split peas
2–3 leeks or scallions
1 bunch fresh parsley, chopped
1 pound fresh beet greens or spinach, chopped
a few sprigs fresh cilantro, chopped (optional)
10–15 pitted prunes

1 tablespoon sugar

a few sprigs fresh mint, chopped, or 1
  tablespoon dried mint

1 tablespoon butter

Brown the onion in the butter or shortening in a large pot. Add the water, rice, turmeric, salt, pepper, yellow split peas, leeks or scallions, parsley, beet greens or spinach, and cilantro. Bring to a boil, lower the heat, cover, and simmer for 30 minutes. Add the prunes and sugar and simmer another 30 minutes. Sauté the chopped mint in butter and sprinkle it over the top just before serving.

If desired, this soup may be prepared with a whole chicken. If so, the total cooking time should be 1 1/2 hours. The chicken may be removed before serving, cooled and boned, then returned to the soup. Alternatively, tiny meatballs can be dropped into the soup during the last 30 minutes of cooking.

---

MEATBALL SOUP (Ashe-e Sak)

*Serves 6–8*

1 large onion, chopped

1 tablespoon butter or shortening

1 pound fresh spinach, chopped

1 fresh beet, peeled and chopped
1/2 cup chopped parsley
2–3 leeks, chopped
3 quarts water (or more)
1 tablespoon turmeric
3 teaspoons salt
1/4 teaspoon pepper
3/4 cup dried yellow split peas
1 small onion, grated
1 package dried onion soup mix
1 teaspoon turmeric
1/4 teaspoon pepper
1/2 pound lean ground beef
2 tablespoons butter or shortening
1 cup rice flour
1/2 cup cold water
1 cup sour grape juice or 2/3 cup lemon juice
1/4 cup ground walnuts (optional)
yogurt (optional)
3–4 eggs (optional)

Sauté the chopped onion in the butter or shortening until brown. Cook the spinach, beet, parsley, and leeks for 5 minutes in water to cover; drain; add to the onions. Add the water, turmeric, salt, pepper, and yellow split peas. Cover and simmer for 30 minutes. Meanwhile, combine the grated onion, instant dried onion soup mix, turmeric, pepper, and ground beef. Mix together well with the hands and shape into tiny meatballs, about the size of small cherries. Brown these meatballs in the butter or shortening. Drop them into the soup, cover, and continue simmering for another 30 minutes. Using a wire whisk, mix together the rice flour and cold water, making a smooth paste. Pour this paste slowly into the soup, stirring constantly. Add the sour grape or lemon juice. Simmer a few more minutes. Ground walnuts may be sprinkled over the top just before serving. The soup may be served plain or with yogurt. If adding yogurt, first spoon a few tablespoons of the hot soup into the yogurt to warm it, then stir the yogurt into the soup. Another possibility would be to beat 3 or 4 eggs and pour them gradually into the soup, stirring continuously, a few minutes before serving.

# *Persian Soufflés*

### GREEN HERB KOOKOO
  (Kookoo-ye Sabzi)
  *Serves 6*
  *This Persian omelette will taste best if it is prepared with fresh herbs (sabzi).*

1 cup chopped leeks or scallions (including half the green stems)
a few lettuce leaves, chopped
1/2 cup chopped spinach
1/2 cup chopped fresh dill weed
1 cup chopped parsley
1/4 cup chopped cilantro
2 tablespoons butter or shortening
8 eggs
1/2 teaspoon baking soda
1/2 teaspoon turmeric or saffron
1/8 teaspoon cinnamon
1/2 teaspoon salt
1/4 teaspoon pepper
3 tablespoons chopped walnuts (optional)
3 tablespoons dried currants (optional)
yogurt

Sauté the leeks or scallions, lettuce, spinach, dill weed, parsley, and cilantro for 5 minutes in 1 tablespoon of the butter or shortening, stirring frequently. Beat the eggs well. Add the baking soda, turmeric or saffron, cinnamon, salt, and pepper. Add the sautéed greens. Melt the remaining 1 tablespoon of butter or shortening in a skillet and pour in the egg mixture. Do not stir. Cook over medium heat until well browned. Lift the edge of the *kookoo* with a spatula to see if it is brown; then turn it over (as you would turn a large pancake) and brown the other side. (An easier method is to melt the remaining butter or shortening in an oblong Pyrex dish, pour in the egg mixture, and bake in a 350° oven for 45 to 60 minutes, or until the *kookoo* is crisp on the bottom and light brown on the top.) Serve with yogurt. To make this a festive dish, add 3 tablespoons of chopped walnuts and/or currants. This *kookoo* may be eaten either hot or cold.

# Rice Dishes

RICE (Chello)

*Serves 4–6*

*3 cups rice (American long-grain)*
*6 tablespoons salt*
*4 tablespoons butter or shortening*

Bring a large pot of water to a rolling boil. Pour in the rice and salt. Stir once. Boil hard for exactly 10 minutes. Pour the rice into a large colander; rinse well under cold water and drain. Melt the butter or shortening in a saucepan over medium heat. Pour in the rice. Place a dish towel over the inside of the lid, bring the overlapping edges up over the top of the lid, and tie the corners. Cover the saucepan with the wrapped lid. (The cloth absorbs the moisture, preventing the drops of water that ordinarily form on the inside of the lid from dropping back into the rice and making it soggy.) Steam the rice over medium heat for 20 to 25 minutes or over medium-low heat for 30 to 35 minutes. The rice will be ready when, upon lifting the lid, a cloud of steam emerges from the saucepan. The heat can then be turned very low and the rice kept warm until ready to serve.

Always dish out the rice with a slotted spoon, fluffing it as you place it in a serving dish. A crust of *tah-dig* (literally, "bottom-of-the-pan") will have formed on the bottom of the saucepan. To serve this in one unbroken piece, immerse the exterior of the pan in cold water for a few minutes. Pry the *tah-dig* loose with a spatula. A more exotic variety of *tah-dig* can be made by mixing 1 cup of the par-boiled rice with 1/4 teaspoon of saffron and 3 tablespoons of yogurt; spread this over the melted butter or shortening in the bottom of the saucepan. Or, best of all, place two or three thin layers of Lebanese mountain bread (also known as flatbread, or *lavash*) in the melted butter or shortening in the bottom of the saucepan before adding the rice. This makes a crisp delicacy fit for a king.

If you are using Persian long-grain rice (*domsiah*), rinse it very well until the water runs clear. Soak it in plain or salted water for several hours or overnight. When cooking, follow the directions given above, but reduce the boiling time to 5 minutes.

### RICE WITH LENTILS (Adas Pollo)

*Serves 4–5*

*3 cups rice*
*6 tablespoons salt*
*3/4 cup dried lentils*
*1/4 cup butter or shortening*

Bring a large kettle of water to a rolling boil. Add the rice and salt. Boil 10 minutes. Pour the rice into a colander, rinse with cold water, and set aside to drain well. Boil the lentils in enough salted water to cover for about 10 minutes; they should be tender but not soft. Drain. Melt the butter or shortening in a large pot. Pour in 1/3 of the rice. Sprinkle with 1/3 of the lentils. Continue alternating layers of rice and lentils. Cover with a lid that has been wrapped in a cloth and steam over medium heat for 30 minutes.

For a more elegant dish, add 1/4 cup toasted, slivered almonds and 1/4 cup currants or raisins just before steaming.

---

### RICE WITH LENTILS AND CHICKEN (Adas Pollo ba Morgh)

*Serves 4–6*
*Follow the recipe above for Rice with Lentils*

up until the butter or shortening is melted in
a large pot. Set it aside and prepare the
following:

1/4 cup butter or shortening
1 large fryer chicken, cut up, or 6 chicken
    breasts
1 large onion, chopped
1 teaspoon turmeric
1 15-ounce can chicken bouillon or consommé
3 tablespoons lemon juice
1 tablespoon tomato paste
1/4 cup warm water
2 tablespoons soy sauce
1/2 teaspoon salt
1/4 teaspoon pepper
1–2 tablespoons flour (optional)
toasted almonds (optional)
dried currants or raisins (optional)

Preheat the oven to 325°. Melt the butter or
shortening in a skillet and brown the chicken
pieces on all sides. Remove them from the
pan. Brown the onion. Stir in the turmeric.
Return the chicken pieces to the pan. Add the
bouillon or consommé, lemon juice, tomato
paste (dissolved in the warm water), soy sauce,
salt, and pepper. Cover and bake for 2 hours,
turning the pieces occasionally. Remove from

the oven and cool. Bone and skin the chicken. The drippings may be thickened with 1 or 2 tablespoons of flour.

After melting 1/4 cup butter or shortening in a large pot, pour in 1/4 of the rice. Place 1/3 of the chicken on top, with several spoonfuls of drippings. Sprinkle over this 1/3 of the lentils and (if desired) toasted almonds and dried currants or raisins. Continue alternating layers until the ingredients have all been used up, finishing with a layer of rice. Pour any remaining drippings over the top. Cover with a lid wrapped in a cloth and steam over medium heat for 30 minutes.

If desired, just before serving dissolve 1/4 teaspoon of powdered saffron in 2 teaspoons of hot water. Mix with several tablespoons of cooked rice. Sprinkle this over the top. Serve the bottom crust separately.

---

SWEET RICE (Shirin Pollo)
*Serves 4−6*
*14 tablespoons butter or shortening*
*1 large fryer chicken, cut up*
*2 1/2 teaspoons saffron*
*1 15-ounce can chicken bouillon or consommé*

3 tablespoons lemon juice

1 tablespoon tomato paste

1/4 cup hot water

1/2 teaspoon salt

1/4 teaspoon pepper

2 cups carrots cut into thin, 1-inch-long strips

1/2 cup water

1 tablespoon sugar

3–4 ounces pistachios in the shell or 1/2 cup
  slivered or whole pistachios

1 cup orange marmalade

1/2 cup slivered almonds

1 cup water

3 cups rice

6 tablespoons salt

Melt 6 tablespoons of the butter or short-ening in a skillet and brown the chicken pieces on all sides. Stir in 1/2 teaspoon of the saffron; add the bouillon or consommé, lemon juice, tomato paste (dissolved in the hot water), salt, and pepper. Cover and simmer gently over low heat for about 1 hour or cover and place in a slow oven (325°) for 2 hours. Cool and bone.

Boil the carrots in the water to which the sugar has been added. When tender, drain and sauté the carrots in 2 tablespoons of the butter or shortening. Shell the pistachios and soak them for a few minutes in warm water; with a sharp knife, cut them into thin slivers. (The pistachios can be left whole or purchased already slivered.) Add these to the carrots. Add the marmalade, slivered almonds, the remaining saffron, and the water. Simmer these ingredients together, uncovered, for 15 minutes.

Bring a large kettle of water to a rolling boil. Add the rice and salt. Boil for 10 minutes; drain, rinse with cold water, and set aside to drain well. Melt the remaining 6 tablespoons of butter or shortening in a large pan and pour in 1/3 of the rice. Arrange half the chicken pieces over this, then add several spoonfuls of the carrot-marmalade mixture. Cover with 1/3 more of the rice, then the rest of the chicken and carrot-marmalade mixture. Cover with the remaining rice. Pour the chicken drippings over the top. Cover with a lid wrapped in a cloth and steam for about 30 minutes over medium-low heat. This dish may be kept warm over very low heat until ready to serve. Serve the bottom crust separately. This dish may also be baked, covered, in the oven at 350° for 1 hour.

To prepare the orange marmalade from

scratch, boil 1 cup of slivered orange peel in
4 cups of water for a few minutes, then pour
the water off. Repeat. Soak the orange slivers
in 4 cups of water for 24 hours. Boil 2 cups of
sugar with 3/4 cup of water for 5 minutes.
Drain the orange slivers and add to the syrup.
Boil until it thickens, stirring constantly to
prevent burning.

---

## DILL WEED RICE WITH FAVA BEANS AND LAMB (Baghali Pollo)

*Serves 4–6*

*2 large onions, sliced or chopped*
*1/2 cup butter or shortening*
*5 lamb shanks*
*1 teaspoon turmeric*
*1/4 teaspoon cinnamon (optional)*
*1 15-ounce can beef broth*
*3 tablespoons lemon juice*
*2 tablespoons tomato paste*
*1/4 cup hot water*
*3 cups rice*
*6 tablespoons salt*
*1 cup fresh dill weed, chopped, or 4–5
    tablespoons dried dill weed*
*1 1/2 cups fresh fava beans, or 3/4 cup dried*

> fava beans, or 1 12-ounce package frozen
> lima beans
1/2 teaspoon saffron
2 teaspoons hot water
yogurt

Preheat the oven to 350°. Sauté the onions in 4 tablespoons of the butter or shortening until brown. Add the lamb shanks and brown well on all sides. Place these in a heavy, ovenproof dish. Stir in the turmeric and cinnamon (if used). Add the beef broth, lemon juice, and tomato paste (diluted in the hot water). Cover and braise in the oven for 2 1/2 hours. Cool and bone the shanks.

Bring a large pot of water to a rolling boil. Add the rice and salt. If dried dill weed is used, add it to the water. Boil for 10 minutes; drain, rinse well with cold water, and drain again.

If using dried fava beans, soak them for 3 hours before boiling. They will require a much longer time to cook than fresh fava beans. Boil the fava beans in salted water until done but still firm (about 10 to 15 minutes for fresh beans and about 45 minutes for soaked dried beans). Drain off the hot water; cool by covering the beans with cold water.

Skin the fresh beans by pressing each bean on one edge so that it will slip out of its skin (dried fava beans do not have this skin). If using lima beans, boil as directed on the package; remove from the heat while the beans are still firm. Cool and peel.

Melt the remaining 4 tablespoons of butter or shortening in a large pot. Add 1/3 of the rice. If fresh dill is used, sprinkle some of it over the rice. Cover with 1/3 of the beans, then 1/3 of the meat. Alternate layers until the ingredients are all used up. Cover the pot with a lid wrapped in a cloth and steam over medium heat for 30 minutes or until the rice is done. Just before serving, dilute the saffron in the hot water. Mix this with 1 cup of the cooked rice. Sprinkle this saffron-colored rice over the top.

This dish may also be prepared with stewed chicken. If you wish, thicken the meat drippings with a little flour and serve in a gravy boat. This dish is traditionally served with yogurt.

## RICE WITH BAKED LAMB
## OR CHICKEN (Tah-Chin)

*Serves 6–8*

*The name for this dish means, literally, "ar-ranged on the bottom of the pan." It can be prepared with either lamb or chicken. If you use lamb, try to obtain a young spring lamb or New Zealand lamb.*

*3–4 pounds leg of lamb or 1 large fryer chicken*
*2 cups yogurt*
*2 large onions, chopped*
*2 teaspoons saffron*
*1 teaspoon turmeric (optional)*
*2 tablespoons soy sauce*
*2 tablespoons lemon juice*
*1 teaspoon salt*
*1/4 teaspoon pepper*
*4 cups rice*
*8 tablespoons salt*
*2 egg yolks*
*1/2 cup butter or shortening*
*2 teaspoons hot water*

Marinate the lamb or chicken overnight in a sauce made by combining the yogurt, on-ions, 1 teaspoon of the saffron, turmeric (if used), soy sauce, lemon juice, salt, and pep-per. Preheat the oven to 325°. Remove the meat from the marinade and reserve the marinade. Bake the meat for 2 hours or until done. Cool and bone.

Bring a large pot of water to a rolling boil. Add the rice and salt; stir just once. Boil 10 minutes; drain in a colander, rinse with cold water, and drain again. Mix 2 cups of the parboiled rice with the marinade and beaten egg yolks. Melt 4 tablespoons of the butter or shortening in a pan and spread the rice mixture in the melted butter or shortening over the bottom of the pan. Arrange the baked lamb or chicken over this and cover with the rest of the rice. Cover with a lid that has been wrapped in a dish towel and steam over medium-low heat for 45 minutes.

Dissolve the remaining teaspoon of saffron in hot water. Stir 1/2 cup of the cooked rice into the saffron water until golden. After arranging the rice and meat on a serving platter, garnish with the saffron rice. Melt the remaining 4 tablespoons of butter or shortening and pour over the top.

For a variation of this recipe known as Tah-Chin Esfenaj, boil 1 pound fresh or 1 package frozen spinach until tender. After spreading the rice mixture over the bottom of the pan, spread the cooked spinach over the rice. Arrange the meat or chicken over the spinach, then place 10 pitted prunes or dried apricots over the meat and cover with the rest of the rice. Proceed as indicated.

# *Stewed Meats*

CHICKEN OR LAMB IN
   POMEGRANATE SAUCE
   (Khoresht-e Fesenjan)
   *Serves 6–8*
*2 large onions, chopped or sliced*
*5 tablespoons butter or shortening*
*1 large fryer chicken or 5 whole chicken breasts*
*1/2 teaspoon poultry seasoning*
*1 15-ounce can beef bouillon or consommé*
*1 cup water*
*2 1/2 cups finely ground walnuts*
*4–5 tablespoons pomegranate syrup*
*2–3 tablespoons sugar*
*2–3 teaspoons salt*
*1/2 teaspoon saffron or turmeric*
*1/4 teaspoon cinnamon*
*1/4 teaspoon nutmeg*
*2 tablespoons lemon juice*
*cooked rice*

   Sauté the onions in 2 tablespoons of the butter or shortening until brown. Remove from

the pan. Add the remaining butter or shortening, season the chicken with poultry seasoning, and brown the chicken pieces. Add
the bouillon or consommé and sautéed onions. Cover and simmer gently for 30 minutes. Cool and bone.

Prepare the sauce by stirring the water
into the ground walnuts. Stir in the pomegranate syrup and sugar and simmer gently over
low heat for 10 to 15 minutes. Combine the
cooked chicken with the walnut sauce. Add
the seasonings and the lemon juice; cover and
simmer gently for another hour. Adjust the
seasonings by adding a little sugar if too sour
or more pomegranate syrup if too sweet. The
chicken pieces should be coated with a rich,
dark, sweet-sour sauce; there should be plenty
of thick sauce. Serve with rice.

This *khoresht* may also be made with meatballs (from ground beef) or lamb (cut into 1-
inch cubes).

For another variation of this recipe, reduce
the sugar to 1 tablespoon and increase the
lemon juice to 4 tablespoons. Substitute 2–3
tablespoons of tomato paste for the pomegranate syrup. Or, substitute 5 tablespoons of

undiluted frozen orange juice for the pomegranate syrup.

---

STEWED LAMB WITH SPINACH
AND PRUNES
(Khoresht-e Esfenaj va Aloo)
*Serves 6*

*2–3 pounds shoulder of lamb or 6 lamb shanks
or beef short ribs*
*3 large onions, chopped*
*2–3 tablespoons butter or rendered fat*
*1 teaspoon turmeric*
*1 15-ounce can beef broth or bouillon*
*1/4 cup lemon juice*
*1/2 cup water*
*2 teaspoons salt*
*1/4 teaspoon pepper*
*1 tablespoon dried leaf fenugreek*
*2 pounds fresh spinach or 2 12-ounce packages
frozen chopped spinach*
*4 bunches scallions, chopped*
*10–12 pitted prunes*
*cooked rice*

Have the butcher bone the shoulder of lamb.
Trim off the fat and cut the meat into stewing-

size pieces. If using lamb shanks or beef short ribs, do not bone; use whole. Sauté the onions in the butter or rendered fat until brown. Add the meat and brown. Stir in the turmeric, beef broth or bouillon, lemon juice, water, salt, pepper, and leaf fenugreek. Cover and simmer over low heat for 1 1/2 hours. If using fresh spinach, wash and drain; chop coarsely. If using frozen spinach, do not defrost. Add the spinach, scallions, and prunes for the last 30 minutes of cooking. Serve with rice.

---

STEWED CHICKEN WITH
  TANGERINES (Khoresht-e Narengi)
  *Serves 6*

*2 large onions, chopped*

*4 tablespoons butter or shortening*

*1 stewing chicken*

*1 teaspoon saffron*

*1 15-ounce can beef or chicken bouillon*

*1/4 cup water*

*1–2 teaspoons salt*

*1/4 teaspoon pepper*

*4 tablespoons lemon juice*

*1/2 pound carrots*

*1/2 cup candied orange or tangerine peel*

*1 tablespoon flour*
*3 tangerines or 2 11-ounce cans mandarin*
   *orange segments*
*4 tablespoons slivered almonds and pistachios*
   *or just almonds*
*cooked rice*

Sauté the onions in the butter or shortening until brown. Add the chicken, whole or cut up, and brown on all sides. Stir in the saffron. Add the bouillon, water, salt, pepper, and lemon juice. Cover and simmer over low heat for 1 hour.

Peel the carrots and slice into thin, 1-inch-long slivers. Add them, together with the candied orange or tangerine peel, to the chicken. Continue simmering until the peel is tender. Thicken the sauce with the flour, using a wire whisk to prevent lumps. Peel the tangerines, separate into segments, and peel each segment. Add them to the stewed chicken. If using mandarin oranges, drain off the liquid and add. To serve, sprinkle with almonds and pistachios. Serve with rice.

---

## DUCKLING IN POMEGRANATE-WALNUT SAUCE (Fesenjan-e Ordak)

*Serves 8–10*

*2 large onions, chopped or sliced*
*4 tablespoons butter or shortening*
*2 ducklings, cut up*
*1 cup beef or chicken bouillon or consommé*
*2 tablespoons lemon juice*
*1/4 cup water*
*1–2 teaspoons salt*
*1/4 teaspoon pepper*
*1/4 teaspoon nutmeg (optional)*
*6 tablespoons pomegranate syrup*
*3–4 tablespoons sugar*
*2 1/2 cups finely ground walnuts*
*cooked rice*

Sauté the onions in the butter or shortening until brown. Remove them from the pan. Brown the duckling pieces on all sides. Return the sautéed onions to the pan. Add the bouillon or consommé, lemon juice, water, salt, pepper, and nutmeg (if used). Cover and simmer gently for 45 minutes. Cool and bone the ducklings. Skim the excess fat off the surface of the cooking liquid. Stir in the pomegranate syrup, sugar, and ground walnuts. Return the boned duckling to the pot, cover, and simmer gently for 1 hour or longer. If necessary, more bouillon, consommé, or water may be added. If desired, the duckling may be cooked in a 350° oven for the last hour. Uncover the pan and continue cooking another 20 to 30 minutes. The sauce will become quite dark. Serve with rice.

# Grilled Meats

## SHISH KABOB

*Serves 4*

Have the butcher bone a 3-pound shoulder of lamb. Cut the meat into 2-inch cubes, trimming off some (but not all) of the excess fat. Marinate overnight in one of the marinades listed for Fillet of Lamb Kabob. Place the meat on skewers, alternating it with cherry tomatoes.

Cook the meat over a charcoal fire until brown on one side; turn the skewers over and brown the other side. Serve with fluffy white rice with butter, rice with lentils, or any other rice dish. Have little bowls of ground sumac (if available) on the table for sprinkling over the kabobs and rice.

## FILLET OF LAMB KABOB
### (Kabab-e Barg)
*Serves 4*

*2–3 pounds lamb fillets or 3 pounds shoulder of
lamb cut into large cubes*

*(1)*

*3 tablespoons vegetable oil*
*1 large onion, chopped or grated*
*1 tablespoon soy sauce*
*1 teaspoon worcestershire sauce*
*1 package dried onion soup mix*

*(2)*

*2 cups yogurt*
*1 large onion, grated, chopped, or sliced*

*(3)*

*2/3 cup vinegar*
*2 large onions, chopped*
*1 tablespoon oregano*
*1/2 cup pale dry cocktail sherry or 3
tablespoons lemon juice*

Marinate the lamb in one of the three marinades for at least 24 hours. Cook on a grill
over a charcoal fire until brown on one side.

47

Turn and brown the other side. Season to taste with salt and pepper.

The kabobs are traditionally served with rice, and raw egg yolks may be stirred into the rice while it is still hot. If available, ground sumac is sprinkled over the kabobs and rice.

---

CHICKEN KABOB (Kabab-e Joojeh)

*Serves 6–8*
*2 small fryer chickens*
*6 tablespoons salad oil*
*1 teaspoon saffron*
*1 tablespoon soy sauce*
*3 tablespoons lemon juice*
*1 package dried onion soup mix*
*1 teaspoon salt*
*1/4 teaspoon pepper*
*1/4 teaspoon nutmeg*
*1/4 teaspoon cinnamon*
*(or instead of the nutmeg and cinnamon use*
*1/2 teaspoon paprika and 1 teaspoon poultry*
*seasoning)*

Cut the chickens into serving pieces. Mix all the other ingredients together in a small bowl. Brush the chicken parts with this marinade and set aside for 2 hours at room temperature. Cook them over a charcoal fire for 1 hour. As the chicken is cooking, brush with any leftover marinade. This chicken may also be broiled. Marinate as above and broil for 1 hour on the lowest rack of the oven, turning 2 or 3 times.

The chickens may also be roasted whole. Marinate, then roast in a 350° oven for 2 hours, basting occasionally and turning once after 1 hour of roasting.

---

GROUND BEEF KABOB
  (Kabab-c Koobideh)
  *Serves 4*
*1 1/2 pounds ground beef*
*1 package dried onion soup mix*
*1 large onion, grated*
*1/2 teaspoon seasoning salt*
*1/2 teaspoon cinnamon*
*1/2 teaspoon oregano*
*1/4 teaspoon garlic salt*

Mix all the ingredients well with your hands. Shape into long, narrow strips (about 12 inches long by 2 inches wide) or into individual servings (about 3 inches long by 2 inches wide—

somewhat like elongated hamburger patties).
Cook on a grill over hot coals, turning once,
until brown on both sides.

If using skewers, they should be wide (1 inch
in diameter). Also, 1/2 teaspoon baking soda
and 1 egg should be added to the meat mixture to help hold it together around the skewers. The meat mixture should be refrigerated
until cold. With wet hands, press the meat
firmly around each skewer so that each one is
coated with meat along its entire length except for the ends. Refrigerate until ready to
cook. The charcoal should be very hot, and
the meat should be cooked quickly so that it
will not fall off the skewers.

---

## LEG OF LAMB KABOB
(Kabab-e Ran-e Bareh)
*Serves 8*
*1 leg of lamb*
*1 cup rice*
*10–15 chicken livers*
*2 large onions, chopped*
*3 tablespoons butter or shortening*
*2 tablespoons tomato paste*
*1/2 cup hot water*

2 teaspoons lemon juice

4 tablespoons slivered almonds

4 tablespoons slivered pistachios

2 tablespoons candied orange peel,
   cut in thin strips

2–3 cloves garlic, slivered

Have your butcher bone the leg of lamb.
Boil the rice in salted water for 15 minutes;
drain and set aside. Cut each chicken liver in
half. Sauté the onions in the butter or shortening until brown. Add the chicken livers and
brown. Dilute the tomato paste in the hot
water and pour over the livers. Add the lemon
juice, slivered almonds and pistachios, and
candied orange peel; cover and simmer gently
for 15 minutes. Stir in the drained rice.

Preheat the oven to 325°. Fill the leg of
lamb with the stuffing, roll it up, and truss
well with string. Secure the ends well so that
the stuffing will not spill out. Prick the outer
skin in several fatty places and insert slivers
of garlic under the skin. They may be removed just before serving. Roast the lamb in
the oven for 3 hours, or roast over a charcoal
fire on a rotating spit until done.

# Desserts

---

## PERSIAN COOKIES
(Nan-e Shirini-ye Khoshk)
*Makes about 30 cookies*
*This is a basic recipe which can be varied by
using different flavorings.*

1 1/2 cups butter
1 1/2 cups confectioners' sugar
1 teaspoon vanilla extract, or 2 tablespoons
  cocoa, or 1 teaspoon cinnamon, or grated
  lemon or orange rind
4 cups flour
1 egg yolk or egg white, beaten (optional)
slivered almonds, ground walnuts, or ground
  pistachios (optional)

Beat the butter and confectioners' sugar together until creamy. Add the vanilla extract
or other flavoring. Add the flour and blend
well. Refrigerate for a couple of hours. Preheat the oven to 350°. Roll out the dough between sheets of waxed paper to the desired
thickness. With floured cookie cutters, cut

the dough into the shapes desired. Place on greased cookie sheets and bake for 10 to 12 minutes, depending upon the thickness of the cookies. If desired, the tops may be brushed with beaten egg yolk or egg white before baking and/or sprinkled with slivered almonds, ground walnuts, or ground pistachios.

---

BLOSSOM COOKIES (Nan-e Shokoofeh)
  *Makes about 30 cookies*
*1 1/2 cups butter*
*1 1/2 cups confectioners' sugar*
*4 cups flour*
*1/2 teaspoon almond extract*
*2 egg whites, beaten (optional)*
*3 tablespoons poppy seeds (optional)*

Beat the butter and confectioners' sugar together until creamy. Work the flour in gradually, blending until smooth. Stir in the almond extract. Place this dough in a plastic bag and refrigerate for 24 hours. Preheat the oven to 350°. Shape the dough into small balls. If desired, these may be flattened down somewhat with the back of a fork; the tops may be brushed with beaten egg whites and sprinkled with poppy seeds. Bake on a greased cookie sheet for 15 minutes, then lower the heat to 300° and bake 15 minutes longer, or until the cookies are golden brown.

# Cold Sweet Drinks

ORANGE SYRUP (Sharbat-e Porteghal)

*3 cups orange juice*
*2 pounds sugar*
*grated rind of 1 orange*

Use only a porcelain or enamel pan. Boil the orange juice and sugar together for 20 to 25 minutes, or until the mixture thickens. Add the orange rind and boil gently for a few minutes longer. Strain the liquid through a cheesecloth into a bowl. Cool and bottle. To serve, add water and ice to taste.

LEMON SYRUP (Sharbat-e Ab-Limoo)

*5 pounds sugar*
*6 cups water*
*2 cups lemon juice*
*grated rind of 2 lemons*

Use only a porcelain or enamel pan. Boil the sugar and water together until the mixture starts to thicken. Add the lemon juice and rind; continue boiling until the syrup has a fairly thick consistency. Cool and bottle. To serve, pour a few tablespoons into a glass and add water and ice.

---

QUINCE-LEMON SYRUP
  (Sharbat-e Beh-Limoo)
*2 large quinces*
*2 pounds sugar*
*2 cups water*
*1/4 cup lemon juice*

Use only a porcelain or enamel pan. Peel, quarter, and core the quinces. Grate or chop them very fine. Boil the sugar and water together for 15 to 20 minutes, or until the mixture starts to thicken. Add the quinces and boil 15 minutes longer. Add the lemon juice, simmer briefly, and strain the syrup through a cheesecloth into a bowl. Cool and bottle. To serve, pour a few tablespoons into a glass and add water and ice.

---

SOUR CHERRY SYRUP
  (Sharbat-e Albaloo)
*2 pounds sugar*
*2−3 cups water*

*1 pound fresh sour cherries*
*1/4 teaspoon vanilla extract*

Use only a porcelain or enamel pan. Boil the sugar and water together for 15 to 20 minutes. Add the sour cherries and boil gently another 20 to 30 minutes, or until the syrup thickens. Strain the liquid into a bowl through a cheesecloth, squeezing the cherries to extract all the liquid. Add the vanilla extract. Bottle. To serve, add water and ice.

Dried sour cherries may be used instead of fresh ones. They should be soaked in cold water 6 hours or longer.

# The
# Khwan
# Niamut

THE

# KHWAN NIAMUT;

OR,

*Nawab's Domestic Cookery:*

BEING A SELECTION

OF THE BEST APPROVED

*RECIPES,*

Of the most Flavoured and Savoury

D I S H E S,

FROM THE KITCHEN OF

NAWAB QASIM ULI KHAN,

*Buhadur Qâum Jung.*

FROM THE ORIGINAL PERSIAN.

Calcutta:

*Printed at the Columbian Press, No. 5,
Doomtollah.*

1839.

# Preface.

---

THE *following Sheets have been*
*translated from a small* **Pamphlet,**
*in the Persian Language, containing*
*Recipes of the most Approved and*
*Savoury Dishes, appertaining to the*
*Kitchen of the* NAWAB QASIM ULEE
KHAN, Buhadoor Qáum Jung.—*The*
*Translator hopes, that this Attempt*
*to provide for the best* HINDOOSTNEE.
DISHES *to the* European Community,
*will meet with the Public Favour and*
*Support.*

# TABLE OF WEIGHTS.

---

| 8 | Till......—1 Rice, or Barley Corn, |
|---|---|
| 8 | Rice ....—1 Ruttee—8 ditto, |
| 8 | Ruttees ..—1 Masha, |
| 12 | Mashas ..—1 Tola, or Sicca Weight, |
| $2\frac{1}{3}$ | Ditto, ....—1 Dram, |
| $4\frac{1}{2}$ | Ditto, ....—1 Misqal, |
| $3\frac{1}{2}$ | Misqal....—1 Qeerat. |

---

| 5 | Tolas ....—1 Chuttack, |
|---|---|
| 16 | Chuttacks —1 Seer, |
| 40 | Seers ....—1 Maund. |

---

N. B.—1 Seer is equal to 2 Pounds.

# Table of Contents.

---

# Appendix.

---

# THE
# KHWAN NIAMUT;

OR,

## *Nawab's Domestic Cookery.*

--->+<---

### *Ukhnee Poolao.*

TAKE of Rice, (*Istuemalee*) 1 *seer*,
    Ghee, 1 *seer* and 4 *chuttacks*,
    Salt, 2 *chuttacks*,
    Kid, *one*,
    Beef, 4 *seers*,
    Almond, pealed and bruised,
      *half seer*,
    Cream, 4 *chuttacks*,
    Milk, *half seer*,
    Butter-Milk, 4 *chuttacks*,

Garlick, 1 *dram*,
Cloves, 2 *drams*,
Cinnamon, 6 *mashas*, and
Lime Juice, 4 *chuttacks*.

Wash the Rice well, and keep it soaked in water; slaughter the Kid, and divide it into pieces of a quarter seer each---The Beef likewise to be cut into small pieces---wash them together eight or nine times, and put them both on fire with six seers of water, clearing it at intervals of the scum arising therefrom. When the Meat becomes tender, heat another vessel on fire, and put in it half a dram of Ghee : after its becoming well heated, put in the whole of the Garlick and a part of the Cardamum ; then take the contents of the first vessel (i. e. the Meat and the Gravy) and put it in the second, and allow the whole to be well cooked until the Meat becomes perfectly tender, and the Gravy reduced to one half the quantity----Then heat another vessel with half a dram of Ghee and a little Cardamum, and pour the Gravy in it through a towel, which having retained for a short time on fire, bring it down----Then select the pieces of the Kid, and wash them with a mixture of the whole of the Butter-milk, one third of the Salt, and ten seers of water---Then take the whole of the Ghee, and heat it on fire, and put it in the remaining Cardamums and Cloves; also half of the Gravy and

the pieces of the Kid: after an ebul-
lition of three or four times, put in
a third of the Salt and the Lime
Juice, and continue it on fire until
the gravy is properly mixed in the
Ghee, then bring it down; then mix
the bruised Almonds with the
Cream and Milk, and put the whole
into the Meat, and let it stand on an
easy Charcoal fire,---Now take the
remaining (half) Gravy, and boil the
Rice in it, adding to it the remaining Salt: after it is half cooked,
strain off the Gravy, and put in the
Cinnamon: then put this Rice into
the vessel containing the Meat, and
place it on a Charcoal-fire, taking
care to cover the mouth of the vessel
with some dough, and in about twenty-five minutes it will be fit for use

## Plain Poolao.

Take of Rice, 1 *seer*,

Ghee, 1 *seer*,

Kid, *one*,

Salt, 2 *chuttacks*,

Cloves, 1 *dram*,

Cardamums, 1 *dram*,

Zeerah, 6 *mashas*,

Pepper, 6 *mashas*,

Butter-Milk, *half seer*,

Cream, 4 *chuttacks*,

Milk, 4 *ditto*,

Onions, 4 *ditto*,

Ginger, 1 *chuttack*,

Divide the Kid into pieces of a quarter seer each, and wash it five or six times : let the Rice also be washed and soaked in water; bruise the Garlick and the Ginger, and pound half of the Salt and spread it on the Meat: then mix well the bruised Garlick and Ginger with the Butter Milk, and apply the whole to the Meat. Now heat the Ghee on fire, and put in the Onions well sliced: when they become perfectly brown put in the Meat gradually into the vessel, and fry it well until the Gravy is well mixed in the Ghee: then put in the Cream and the milk after which the Rice, then the Salt, the Cloves, the Cardamums, the Zeerah and the Pepper, and pour in afterwards either cold or warm water, measuring the quantity according to the state of the Meat: let the operation be continued on a slow fire, and when the

Rice is nearly ready, bring it down and place it on an easy Charcoal-fire. In about twenty-five minutes it will be fit or use.

---

### Khichree Biryan.

Take of Rice, *half seer,*

    Dal, *half seer,*

    Salt, 1 *chuttack,*

    Cloves, 6 *mashas,*

    Cardamums, 6 *ditto,*

    Zeerah, 6 *ditto,*

    Pepper, 6 *ditto,*

    Milk, 4 *chuttacks,*

    Cream, 4 *ditto,*

    Ghee, 12 *ditto,* and

    Onions, 1 *ditto,*

Heat the Ghee on fire, and put in it sliced Onions. Wash the Rice and the Dal together, which put in thee Ghee along with Salt, Cardamums, Zeerah and Pepper, and fry it well, until it assumes a fine brown clour. Then put in water sufficient for its cooking, and when it is half cooked, put in it the Cream and the Milk : after a short time take it down and apply dough to the mouth of the vessel, and place it on an easy Charcoal-fire and in the course of twenty-five minutes it will be fit for use

---

*Kichree Biryan, another method.*
Take of Rice *half seer,*
  Dal, *half ditto,*
  Salt, 1 *chuttack,*
  Onions, 1 *ditto,*

Ghee, **6** *chuttacks,*
Cloves, *half masha,*
Pepper, *half ditto,*
Cardamums, *half ditto, &*
Zeerah, 1 *ditto.*

Slice the Onions and fry it well in the Ghee, until it assumes a good brown colour: then put in the Rice and Dal, (previously washed) together, with the other ingredients, and fry them properly: then pour in water, for its cooking, and when it is ready, bring it down, and apply dough to the mouth of the vessel, leaving it on an easy Charcoal-fire for about twenty-five minutes, and it is fit for eating.

*Quorema, Plain.*

Take of Mutton, 1 *seer*,

 Ghee, *half ditto*,

 Duhee, *(Tyre)*, *half ditto*,

 Salt, 1 *chuttack*,

 Onions, sliced, 4 *ditto*,

 Garlick, 2 *ditto*,

 Cloves 1 *dram*,

 Cardamums, 1 *ditto*,

 Pepper, 1 *chuttack*,

 Almonds, pealed and bruised,

  4 *ditto*,

 Cream, 4 *ditto*,

 Saffron, 4 *mashas*, and

 Juice of 5 Lemons.

Was the Mutton two or three times, mix with it Salt, Butter-Milk and Ginger, then heat the Ghee and fry the sliced Onions in it and when it becomes brown, let in the Mutton. and fry it well, putting in gradually a mixture of the Garlick - water, Then convey in it through a little water the Cloves, Cardamums, and Pepper ; when the Meat becomes tender, put in the Cream and the Almonds, and lastly the Lemon Juice and Saffron. After a short time bring the dish down, and let it rest on an easy Charcoal---fire, and in twenty minutes time it is fit for use.

----

*Vegetable Curries.*

Take of Mutton, 1 *seer,*
    Ghee, *half ditto.*
    Duhee, *(Tyre) half ditto*
    Salt, 1 *chuttack,*
    Ginger, 1 *ditto,*

Coriander, 1 *chuttack*,
Onions, 4 *ditto*,
Garlick, 2 *ditto*,
Pepper, 1 *dram*,
Turmeric, 2 *drams*, and
Saffron, 4 *mashas*.

Having washed the Mutton and applied to it Salt, Duhee, Coriander and a mixture of Ginger-water, heat the Ghee on fire, and let in the Onions duly sliced, which fry until it becomes brown, and convey in it the Turmeric well ground: then throw in the Mutton (previously prepared) and keep frying (adding by degrees a mixture of the Garlick-water,) until the Meat is properly softened, when the Vegetables (of whatever kind you like) are to be

put in and let the whole be cooked
with the addition of little water.—
Lastly, on the dish being ready,
put in a little Lemon Juice, or any
other acid, followed up by the Saffron. Then bring it down, and it is
fit for use.

———

*Kubab Khutaee.*
Take of Mutton, 1 *seer,*
　　　Ginger, 4 *chuttacks,*
　　　Salt, 2 *ditto;*
　　　Onions, 4 *ditto,*
　　　Pepper, 2 *drams,*
　　　Cloves, 1 *ditto,*
　　　Cardamums, small, 1 *ditto,*
　　　Coriander, 1 *chuttack,*
　　　Buttter-Milk, *half seer,*
　　　Cream, 4 *chuttaks,*

Almonds, bruised and pealed,
4 *chuttacks,*
Ghee, *half seer,*
Saffron, 4 *mashas,* and
Juice of 4 Lemons.

Clear the meat well of bones and veins, and mince it very finely, and mix with it Ginger and Onions (duly bruised) and the other ingredients, together with the Saffron made into powder. Then take the Duhee, and tie it close in a Towel, to suffer the water to ooze out; after which mix in it the Cream and Almonds, and put the whole into the minced Meat, with two chuttacks of Ghee, and mix them well together, and make it into small balls. This being done, take the remainder of the Ghee and warm it on fire, and when it is well heated, let in the balls, and keep them frying until they become properly brown. Then bring the vessel down, adding to the balls Lemon-Juice.

---

*Kubab Pursund.*

Take of Mutton, 1 *seer,*
    Ginger, *half ditto,*
    Salt, 1 *chuttack,*
    Pepper, *half ditto,*
    Coriander, 1 *ditto,*
    Onions, 2 *ditto,*
    Saffron, 4 *mashas,*
    Duhee, *(Tyre) half seer,*
    Ghee, 4 *chuttacks,*
    Cream, 4 *ditto,*
    Almonds' 4 *ditto,*

Puneer, *(Cheese)* 2 *Chtks.*

Cloves, 1 *dram,*

Cardamums, 1 *do.* and

Juice of 4 Lemons.

Tie up the Duhee in a towel, that the water may ooze out. Cut the Mutton into small pieces, and apply to it a mixture of Ginger-water, pounded Salt and well ground Onions, and the Coriander, after being parched and ground, together with the Lime Juice and Saffron, then mix the Cream and the Almonds, (pealed and bruised) into the Duhee, which, together with the ghee, apply well to the pieces of the Mutton ; and lastly cover them with the Cheese or Puneer, and tie them with a string, and put them on a spit, and keep, them roasting on a slow charcoal-fire, until they assume a perfect brown colour, when they are ready for the table.

———

### *Kubab, Plain.*

Take of Mutton, 1 *seer,*
  Salt, 1 *chuttack,*
  Ginger, 1 *ditto,*
  Onions, 1 *ditto,*
  Pepper, 2 *drams,*
  Ghee, 2 *chuttacks,*
  Duhee, *(Tyre)* 4 *ditto,* and
  Coriander, 1 *ditto.*

Apply these ingredients to the Mutton, cut in pieces, in the same manner as in the foregoing, and let them be roasted on a slow Charcoal-fire.

*Roast Fowl and other Games.*
Take of Ginger, *half chuttack,*

  Coriander, 4 *ditto,*

  Cloves, 1 *masha,*

  Cardamums, 1 *ditto,* and

  Pepper, 2 *drams.*

Clean the Fowl well, and wound it all over with a Fork, then apply these ingredients, well ground and pounded to the Fowl. Then take some Tyre or Duhee (clearing it of water through a cloth) and mix with it some Cream and Onions; fry them in some Ghee, and apply them to the Fowl, which roast in the manner above directed.

---

*How to roast Fish upon a Spit.*
Take of Fish, *half seer,*

  Ghee, 2 *chuttacks,*

Ginger, 2 *chuttacks,*
Onions, 2 *ditto,*
Duhee, *(Tyre)* 4 *ditto,*
Cream, 1 *ditto,*
Coriander, 2 *pice wt.*
Flour of Gram, *half chuttack,*
Cayenne Pepper, 4 *mashas,*
Cloves, 1 *ditto,*
Cardamums, 1 *ditto,*
Salt, 1 *dram,* and
Juice of 4 Lemons.

Cut the Fish into pieces, which wound with a knife throughout, and wash it well with the Flour of Gram; then pound well the Ginger, Coriander, Salt and Cayenne Pepper, and apply them to the Fish.— Then slice the Onions, and fry them well in Ghee, and apply the

both to the Fish; also the Lime-
Juice, Cloves and Cardamums,
pounded; Duhee, cleared of its
water, and Cream---After this appli-
cation, put in the pieces of the Fish
on spit, and roast them on an easy
Charcoal-fire.

### *Khaginah.*

Take of Fowl Eggs, *ten,*
    Ghee, 6 *chuttacks,*
    Flour of parched Gram, 1
       1 *ditto,*
    Salt, *half chuttack,*
    Pepper, 4 *mashas,*
    Coriander, parched and bruis-
      ed, 1 *dram,*
    Cloves, 1 *masha,*
    Cardamums, 1 *ditto,*
    Onions, 1 *chuttack,* and
    Duhee, (*Tyre*) 2 *chuttacks,*

Bruise and pound well the whole of the ingredients, also clear the water from the Duhee, and mix them together with the Eggs, duly broke, and beat the whole up well, then take the Ghee and heat it well on fire, and pour in it the prepared Eggs, which when done on one side, it should be turned on the other, and then cut it very small with a knife, and it is fit for the Table.

---

### Almond Comfits.

Take of pealed and bruised Almonds four Chuttacks, which dry well in about half a seer of Flour, hen pound it and fry it in the same

Ghee. Having done this, prepare
some Syrup of Sugar-candy, clari-
fying it with the glare of half an
Egg; put in the Syrup, some Milk
and Rose-water; then throw in the
Almonds, and mix up the whole
well, after which bring it down and
cool it; then turn it into Comfits---
apply silver foils on the outside.

---

*How to prepare Lozenges of
Carrots and Sweet Pumpkins.*

Take the Carrots, clean and
bruise them well, and fry them in
half a seer of Butter; then prepare
one seer of Syrup, out of half a
seer of Sugar-candy, and pour it
into the Carrots, placing the same
on fire, and after the whole has ac-

quired a sufficient consistence, put in the Juice of half a Lime, and of Saffron, Musk, and Rose-water two mashas each, also four chuttacks of pealed and bruised Almonds, mix the whole up well, and bring the vessel down, and when the mixture is sufficiently cooled, turn it into lozenges, or as it is called *Luoz*.

---

### *Lemon Pickles.*

Rub the Lemons well upon a stone, and throw them in some water; take an earthen vessel, and put the Lemons in it, with the addition of some Salt, and keep it for two or three days, not forgetting however at intervals to give it a good shake: the water that may

come out of the Lemons, should be
thrown off, and when the Lemons
are becme soft, they should be ex-
posed to the sun upon a clean sheet;
after which, on their appearing to
become ripe, they should be put
either in *Urug-i-Nuanea*, or Vinegar, or the Juice of Lemons, just
as it may suit one's fancy.

### *Mangoe Pickles.*

Peal the Mangoes, and divide
them into halves, clearing them of
their stones; then apply to them
some Salt; keep them in the sun
for two or three days; after which
clean them well with a cloth, then
stuff them with some Garlick and
Ginger, well sliced; also Culuonjee

(Seeds of Onion) and tie them up with some thread, which preserve either in Vinegar, *Urug-i-Nuanea*, Mangoe Juice, or Oil, and keep for some days in the sun.

---

### *Lemon Pickles, Kaghuzee.*

Take one seer of Kaghuzee Lemons, and mix in it of Table-Salt two chuttacks, and let it stand for seven or eight days, then throw off the water oozing out of the Lemons, and wipe them well, and put in four Pice weight of white Salt, then take Juice out of other Lemons, and add two tolas of it, and afterwards put in two chuttacks more of Salt, and expose it to the sun.

## *Cashmerian Chutnee.*

Take ten seers of Mangoes, ridding them of their stones, and pound them well along with the rind; mix in it two chuttacks Ginger, Salt, agreeably to the taste, Cloves one dram, Pepper one dram, Kuluonjee (Seeds of Onion) one dram, Coriander-Seed one dram, Nutmeg six mashas, *Neshasta,* (a preparation from the Wheat) six mashas, Mint one dram, Cinnamon one dram, and *Urug-i-Nuanea* half seer, and expose it to the sun for a period of fifteen days—If the *Urug-i-Nuanea* dries up, put in a little more.

*How to fry Fish, or any other thing.*

Clean the Fish well, then take either of some of the Flour of Gram, Rice or Musoor, and mix in it Garlic, Onions, Ginger, and Salt, well pounded, also some *Tyre*, (Duhee) and Turmeric, which apply to the Fish, and fry it in Ghee.

---

*Baqur-Khanee.*

Take Flour of Wheat, (*Myda*) 1 *sr.*

    Milk, 2 *seers*,

    Ghee, 12 *chuttacks*,

    Lahuoree Salt, *half chuttack*,

    Cream, 4 *ditto*,

    Almonds, 3 *ditto*,

    Duhee, (*Tyre*) for the Leaven, 2 *ditto*,

Cardamums, 2 *mashas*, and Flour for the Leaven, 2 *chuttacks.*

Boil the Milk, and let it cool, put in it the Salt and the *Myda*, and knead it well. Then take the other two chuttacks of *Myda*, put in it two chuttacks of Duhee, *(Tyre)* and the Cardamums, then, the Nutmeg and the Cinna-mon, well grounded, and knead up the whole, until it is leavened: then mix this leaven with the former Flour, and keep kneading until the whole is leavened, then make small Cakes of this preparation, apply Ghee on either side of each Cake, and put one Cake upon the other, and lastly put a cloth till the Ghee is congealed: then flatten the whole by a *Belen*, (roller) and put on a wet towel for an hour. Peal the Almonds, and cut into slice, and apply on the top of the Bread, likewise parched with Sesame seed. Put the Bread upon a plate, and apply *Belun* again, then make in it several scars with a knife, and put it into the oven, where throw on it at intervals a little Milk.

---

*Sheermal.*

Take Myda, 1 *seer*,
     Milk, 2 *seers*,
     Ghee, 6 *chuttacks*,
     Lahouree Salt, *half chuttack*,
     Cream, 2 *ditto*,
     Cardamums, 2 *mashas*,
     Nutmeg, pounded, *one*,

Cinnamon, pounded, 2 *mas-has*, and

Myda, 2 *chuttacks,* for the leaven.

Boil the Milk, cool it, and mix in it well the Salt, then put in the *Myda,* and knead it well. Now take the *Myda* for the leaven, and knead it in the Duhee, (*Tyre*) along with the pounded Cardamum and Cinnamon, when the leaven rises, mix it in the prepared Flour for the Bread, and continue kneading until the whole is leavened : then put in the Cream and the Ghee, and make the Loaf of an oblong form, and bake it under the same operations as observed in *Baqur-Khanee.*

*Nan Thaftan.*

Take Flour of Wheat, 1 *seer,*
    Milk, 2 *seers,*
    Ghee 4 *chuttacks,*
    Cream, 2 *ditto,*
    Almonds, 2 *ditto,*
    Salt, *half ditto,*
    Duhee, *(Tyre)* for the leaven,
      2 *chuttacks,*
    Cardamums, 2 *mashas,*
    Nutmeg, pounded, *one,*
    Cinnamon, 2 mashas,
    Myda, for the leaven, 2 *chut:*
    *tacks.*

N. B.----This is prepared in the
same manner as the preceding.

———

*Mangoe Preserves.*
Clean the Mangoes of the rind,

and divide them into halves, wound-
ing the top with a knife ; then boil
them in Water ; after which boil
them again in a Syrup, prepared
either of Sugar or Candy, and tie
the mouth of the vessel with a towel
for a couple of days---Then prepare
other Syrup, and take out the Mangoes and put in it, throwing away
the first Syrup ; and lastly, put in
the Juice of two or three Lemons.

---

### *Pooree.*

Ṭake Myda, 1 *seer,*
Minced Mutton, 1 *ditto,*
Ghee, 1 *ditto,*
Spices, 9 *mashas,*
Ginger, 1 *chuttack,*
Onions, 4 *ditto,*

Salt, *one and half chuttacks,*
Coriander, 1 *ditto,*
Dried Mangoes, 1 *dttto,*
Pepper, 1 *dram,*
Garlick, *half ckuttack,*
Meat, 6 *mashas* and
Cheese, 2 *chuttacks,*

Wash the Minced Mutton, and put in it the Garlick and the Onions, well bruised, and fry it well with four chuttacks of Ghee. Then bring it down and put in the Spices, the Meat, the Cheese and the Coriander, then knead well the Flour, and make several cakes of it, taking two at a time and putting between them the prepared Minced Meat, and shutting their mouth, and then fry them in the Ghee.

*Khujoor Khaseh.*

Take of Flour, 1 *seer,*

     Sugar, 1 *ditto,*

     Ghee, 1 *ditto,* and

     Milk, 1 *ditto.*

Mix about five dirhums of Ghee in the Flour, and boil it well ; then pour in some Water, and let it rest for an hour, after which put in it the Sugar, and knead off the whole well: then warm the Milk, and put in it the kneaded Flour, which must undergo kneading for about *eighty* minutes again, or until the dough becomes hard enough, to admit of its being turned into any shape you like. Make Dates of it, and fry them in the Ghee, should Cream be desired, let a little *Tyre* accompany the mixture.

———

*Goolgoola.*

Take of Flour, 1 *seer,*
  Sugar, 1 *ditto,*
  Ghee, 1 *ditto,*
  Milk, 1 *ditto,*
  Cinnamon, 2 *mashas,* and
  Leaven of Bread, 2 *drams.*

Mix the *Myda* with leaven, and a little of Milk, and add water sufficient to bring the whole to the consistence of Honey : then put in by degrees Sugar and Milk, and place it on the fire, stirring it with a large spoon, till it becomes of the conistance of Honey, when bring it down, aud after it is cooled, make small balls of it, and fry them in the Ghee,

————

### Persian Mode of preparing Coffee.

The coffee ground, or beaten to an impalpable powder, is preserved by closely pressing it down in a wooden box; and the quantity required for us, is scraped from the surface by means of a wooden spoon. Two small coffee-pots are employed; in one is boiled the water, generally mixed with the remaining coffee of a former meal; in the other is put the fresh powder, which is some times placed near the fire, ʒo become heated before tha boiling water is added to it. The mixture is then boiled two or three times, taking care to pour a few drops of cold water upon it the last time, or to place a cloth dipped in cold water over it ; then it is allowed to subside, and afterwards poured in to the coffee-pot which contained only the boiling water.

N. B.--The quantity of coffee powder necessary to make a fine strong tincture of coffee, may be estimated as one coffee cup of coffee powder, to three dishes of proper coffee liquor for the table.

---

### To preserve Fish or Meat, in the Eastern Manner.

The Indians make a trade of

what they call *Parah Muchlee,*
which is fish cut in small pieces,
with salt and sugared tamarind.
Fish thus preserved may be carried
to sea, and will not be found too
salt.  Meat may also be thus preserved, by throwing away the stone
and strings of the tamarinds, and
adding a small portion of Cayenne
pepper.

———

*To preserve Meat by Treacle.*
This experiment has been suc-
cessfully tried in the following manner :---A gentleman put a piece of
beef into treacle, and turned it
often.  At the end of a month he
ordered it to be washed and boiled,
and had the pleasure to find it quite

good, and more pleasent than the same piece would have been in salt for that time. But the expence of this method must confine it to the opulent.

---

### *To preserve Eggs for a Length of time*

Put an egg for one minute in water just about to boil (it will not in that time be hard) and it will afterwards keep well for a month. Steep one a little while in sweet oil, and it will keep for half a year.

---

### *Manner of preserving Eggs perfectly fresh for Twelve Months.*

Having provided small casks, like

oyster barrels, fill them with fresh
laid eggs; then pour into each cask,
the head of which is supposed to
have been first taken out, as much
cold thick lime-water as will fill up
all the void spaces between the
eggs, and like wise completly cover
them. The thicker the lime-water
is the better, provided it will fill up
all the interstices, and the liquid
at the top of the cask; this done,
lay on the head of the casks lightly.
No farther care is necessary, than
merely to prevent the lime from
growing too hard, by adding, occasionally a little common water on
the surface should it seem so dis-
posed, and keeping the casks from
heat and frost. The eggs, when

taken out for use, are to be washed
from the adhering lime with a little
cold water, when they will have
both the appearance and qualities
of fresh laid eggs, the lime preserving them from shrinking or putri-
dity.

———

*To preserve Biscuit for a length
of time from Putrefaction.*

To preserve biscuit a long time
sweet and good, no other art is
necessary, than stowing it well
baked in casks exactly caulked, and
carefully lined with tin, so as to
exclude the air; at the same time
the biscuit must be so placed as to
leave as little vacant room as pos-

sible in the cask; and when the same is opened through necessity, it must be speedily closed again with great care.

———

## *To preserve Lemon-Juice for many years.*

Care must be taken to squeeze only sound friut, as a tainted lemon will endanger the spoiling of the whole: the expressed juice must be depurated by standing a few days, adding one ounce of cream of tartar to every quart of lemon juice; filter it pretty clear; then it is to be put into small bottles, none of them containing more than a pint of juice; in the neck of the bottle, a little of the best oil of olives is to be poured, and the cork well sealed over.

———

*Improved Method of Salting either Butter or Meat.*

Best common salt two parts, saltpetre one part, sugar one part; beat them up together, so that they may be completely blended. To every sixteen ounces of butter add one ounce of the composition; mix it well in the mass, and close it up for use----It should not be used for a month, that it may be thoroughly incorporated. Butter thus cured, has been kept for three years perfectly sweet. Keep the air from it, or it spoils. Cover it with an oiled paper, and a board on that.

To cure meat, add one ounce of
the above composition to every sixteen ounces of meat.  It must be
*very well rubbed in to the meat.*
You cannot have it too finely
powdered, nor too well rubbed in
to the meat.

------

*To keep Oranges and Lemons,
fresh all the year.*

Take small sand, and make it
very dry ; after it is cold, put a
quantity of it into a clean vessel,
then take your oranges, and set
a laying of them in the same, the
stalk-end downwards, so that they
do not touch each other, and strew
in some of the sand, as much as

will cover them two inches deep ; then set your vessel in a cold place, and you will find your fruit in high preservation at the end of the year.

---

*An excellent Method of Preserving fruit fresh all the Year.*

Take of saltpetre one pound, of bole-armenic two pounds, of common sand, well freed from its earthy parts, four pounds, and mix altogether. After this let the fruit be gathered with the hand, before it be thorough ripe, each fruit being handled only by the stalk ; lay them regularly, and in order, in a large wide mouthed glass vessel ; then cover the top of the glass with an oiled paper, and carrying it into a dry place, set it in a box filled all round, to about four inches thickness, with the aforesaid preparations, so that no part of the glass vessel shall appear, being in a manner buried in the prepared nitre; and at the end of a year such fruits may be taken out, as beautiful as when they were first put in.

------

### Cream Preserved fresh all the Year.

Mix with a quantity of fresh rich cream, half its weigth of white sugar in powder; stir the whole well together, and preserve it in bottles well corked. In this state it is ready to mix with tea or coffee, and has continued in good condition fresh all the year.

## *An excellent Substitute for Milk or Cream.*

When milk or cream cannot be got, it is an excellent substitute to bear up the whole of a fresh egg, in a bason, and then gradually to pour boiling tea over it, to prevent its curding. It is difficult from the taste to distinguish the composition from to and rich cream. This might be of great use at sea, as eggs may be preserved fresh in various ways.

---

## *To make the celebrated Eastern Beverage, called Sherbet.*

This liquor is a species of negus without the wine. It consists of water, lemon or orange juice, and sugar, in which are dissolved per-

fumed cakes, made of the best Da-
mascus fruit; and containing also
an infusion of some drops of rose
water ; another kind is made of
violets, honey, juice of raising, &c.

It is well calculated for assuaging
thirst, as the acidity is agreeably
blended with sweetness. It resem-
bles, indeed, those fruits which we
find so grateful when one is thiristy

---

## To Extract Syrup from Indian Corn.

The yuong spikes, when they are
beginging to form, possess a very
agreeable saccharine taste. Ten
pounds of them squeezed in a stone
mortar, and the juice expressed,
after the leaves are stripped off, will

give about four pounds of a milky juice, which when clarified and evaporated to the consistence of a syrup, will be found very agreeable to the palate. This vegetable will grow in England from the seed, sown in good soil.

---

### Easy Method of producing Mushrooms.

It the water wherein mushrooms have been steeped or washed be poured upon an old bed, or if the broken part of mushrooms be strewed thereon, there will speedily arise great numbers.

---

### To perfume Linen.

Rose leaves dried in the shade, cloves beat to powder, and mace scraped; mix them together, and put the composition into little bags.

END OF KHWAN NIAMUT.

# APPENDIX.

# APPENDIX.

THE FOLLOWING PAGES BEING A SELECTION FROM THE DOMASTIC ECONOMY.

## FISH.

### *Stewed Carp.*

Scale and clean. Lay the fish in a stew-pan, with a rich beefgravy, an onion, eight cloves, a desert-spoonful of peper, a fourth part of the quantity of gravy or part (cyder may do); simmer close-covered; when nearly done add two anchovies chopped fine, a desert-spoonful of made mustard, and some fine wal-

nut-ketchup, a bit of butter rolled
in flour : shake it, and let the gravy
boil a few minutes. Serve with
sippets of fried bread, and a good
deal of horse-radish and lemon.

---

### Boiled Eels.

The small ones are best : do them
in a small quantity of water, with
a good deal of parsley, which should
be served up with them and the
liquor.---Serve chopped parsley and
butter for sauce.

---

### Eel Broth, very nourishing for the Sick

Do as above; but stew two hours,
and add an onion and pepper-corns :
salt to taste.

### Collared Eel.

Bone a large eel, but don't skin it: mix pepper, salt, mace, allspice, and a clove or two, in the finest powder, and rub over the whole inside ; roll it tight, and bind with a coarse tape. Boil in salt and water till enough, then add vinegar, and when cold keep the collar in pickle. Serve it either whole or in slices. Chopped sage, and parsley, mixed with the spices, greatly improve the taste.

### Hot Crab.

Pick the meat out of a crab, clear the shell from the head, then put the meat with a little nutmeg, salt, pepper, a bit of butter, crumbs of

bread, and three spoonsful of vinegar, into the shell again, and set it
before the fire.---Dry toast should be
served to eat it upon.

### Dressed Crab, cold.

Empty the shells, and mix the
flesh with oil, vinegar, salt, and a
little white pepper and Cayenne;
then put the mixture into the large
shell, and serve.    Very little oil is
necessary.

## MEATS.

### To dress Venison.

A haunch of buck will take three
hours and a half, or three quarters,
roasting: doe, only three hours and

a quarter. Venison should be rather
under than over done.

Spread a sheet of white paper
with butter, and put it over the fat,
first sprinkling it with a little salt;
then lay a coarse paste on strong
paper, and cover the haunch; tie
it with fine packthread, and set it
at a distance from the fire, which
must be a good one. Baste it often;
ten minutes before serving take off
the paste, draw the meat nearer the
fire, and baste it with butter and a
good deal of flour, to make it forth
up well.

Gravy for it should be put into
a boat, and not into the dish (un-
less there is none in the venison)
and made thus: Cut off the fat

from two or three pounds of a loin of mutton, and set in steaks on a gridiron for a few minutes just to brown one side; put them into a sauce-pan with a quart of water, cover quite close for an hour, and simmer it gently; then uncover it, and stew till the gravy is reduced to a pint. Season with only salt.

*Sauce.*—Make the jelly-sauce thus: Beat some currant-jelly and a spoonful or two of port wine, and set it over the fire till melted. Where jelly runs short put more wine, and a few lumps of sugar, to the jelly, and melt as above.— Serve with French beans.

### *To salt Beef or Pork, for eating immediately.*

The piece should not weigh more than five or six pounds. Salt it very throughly just before you put it into the pot ; take a coarse cloth, flour it well, put the meat in, and fold it up close. Put it into a pot of boiling water, and boil it as long as you would any other salt beef of the same size, and it will be as if done four or five days.

----

### *To salt Beef red ; which is extremely good to eat fresh from the Pickle, or to hang to dry.*

Choose a piece of beef with as little bone as you can (the flank is most proper), sprinkle it, and let it drain a day; then rub it with common salt, saltpetre, and bay-salt, but only a small proportion of the saltpetre, and you may add a few grains ef cochineal, all in fine powder. Rub the pickle every day into the meat for a week, then only turn it.

---

### An excellent Mode of dressing Beef.

Hang three ribs three or four days; take out the bones from the whole length, sprinkle it with salt, roll the meat tight, and roast it. Nothing can look nicer. The above done with spices, &c. and baked is excellent.

*To dress cold Beef that has not been done enough, called Beef-Olives.*

Cut slices half an inch thick, and four inches square ; lay on them a forcemeat of crumbs of bread, shalot, a little suet, or fat, pepper, and salt. Roll them, and fasten with a small skewer : put them into a stew-pan with some gravy made of the beef-bones, or the gravy of the meat, and a spoonful or two of water, and stew them till tender. Fresh meat will do.

———

*To stew Tongue.*

Salt a tongue with saltpetre and common salt for a week, turning it every day. Boil it tender enough to peel : when done, stew it in a moderately strong gravy ; season with soy, mush-room ketchup, Cayenne, pounded cloves, and salt if necessary.

----

### Beef-heart.

Wash it carefully ; stuff it and serve with rich gravy, and currant-jelly sauce.---Hash with the same, and port wine.

----

### Veal-rolls of either cold Meat or fresh.

Cut thin slices ; and spread on them a fine seasoning of a very few crumbs, a little chopped bacon or scraped ham, and a little suet, some fresh mushrooms stewed and minced, pepper, salt, and a small piece of pounded mace.

This stuffing may either fill up the roll like a sausage, or be rolled with the meat. In either case tie it up very tight, and stew it very slowly in a gravy and a glass of sherry.---Serve it when tender, after skimming it nicely.

### Veal Collops.

Cut long thin collops; beat them well; and lay on them a bit of thin bacon of the same size, and spread forcemeat on that, seasoned high, and also a little garlick and Cayenne. Roll them up tight, about the size of two fingers, but not more than two or three inches long; put a very small skewer to fasten each firmly; rub egg over; fry them of a fine brown, and pour a rich brown gravy over.

———

### To boil a Calf's Head.

Clean it very nicely, and soak it in water, that it may look very white; take out tongue to salt, and the brains to make a litle dish. Boil the head extremely tender; then strew it over with crumbs and chopped parsly, and brown them; or, if liked better, leave one side plain. Bacon and greens are to be served to eat with it.

The brains must be boiled; and then mixed with melted butter, scalded sage chopped, pepper, and salt.

If any of the head is left, it may
be hashed next day and a few slices
of bacon just warmed and put round.

---

### Calf's Liver.

Slice it, season with pepper and
salt, and broil nicely ; rub a bit of
cold butter on it, and serve hot and
hot.

---

### To dress Pork as Lamb.

Kill a young pig of four or five
months old; cut up the fore-quar-
ter for roasting as you do lamb,
and truss the shank close. The
other parts will make delicate pickled pork ; or steaks, pies, &c.

---

### Pork Steaks.

Cut them from a loin or neck,

and of middling thickness; pepper
and broil them, turning them often;
when nearly done, put on salt, rub
a bit of butter over, and serve the
moment they are taken off the fire,
a few at a time.

### Sausages.

Chop fat and lean pork together:
season it with sage, pepper, and
salt, and you may add two or three
berries of allspice: *half fill* hog's
guts that have been soaked and
made extremely clean: or the meat
may be kept in a very small pan,
closely covered: and so rolled and
dusted with a very little flour before
it is fried. Serve on stewed red
cabbage; or mashed potatoes put

in a form, brown with salamander,
and garnish with the above they
must be pricked with a fork before
they are dressed, or they will burst.

---

## *To hash Mutton.*

Cut thin slices of dressed mutton; fat and lean; flour them; have
ready a little onion boiled in two or
three spoonsful of water; add to it a
little gravy and the meat seasoned,
and make it hot, but not to boil.
Serve in a covered dish. Instead
of onion, a clove, a spoonful of cur-
rant) jelly, and half a glass of port
wine, will give an agreeable flavour
of venison, if the meat be fine.

Pickled cucumber, or walnut,
cut small, warm in it for change.

### An excellent Hotch-potch.

Stew peas, lettuce, and onions, in a very little water with a beef or ham-bone. While these are doing, fry some mutton or lamb-steaks seasoned, of a nice brown; three quarters of an hour before dinner, put the steaks into a stewpan, and the vegetables over them; stew them, and serve altogether in a tureen.

*Another.*---Knuckle of veal, and scrag of mutton, stewed with vegetables as above; to both, and a bit of butter rolled in flour.

### To boil Ducks.

Choose a fine fat duck; salt it two days, then boil it slowly in a cloth. Serve it with onion-sauce, but melt the butter with milk instead of water.

---

### To hash Ducks.

Cut a cold duck into joints; and warm it, without boiling in gravy, and a glass of port wine.

---

## SOUPS, &c.

---

### Veal broth.

Stew a small kuckle in about three quarts of water, two ounces of rice, a little salt, and a blade of mace, till the liquor is half wasted away.

---

### Sauce for Fowl of any sort.

Boil some veal-gravy, pepper,

salt, the juice of an orange and a lemon, and a quarter as much of port wine as of gravy, and pour it into the dish, or a boat.

———

### Onion Sauce.

Peel the onions, and boil them tender : squeeze the water from them, then chop them, and add to them butter that has been melted rich and smooth, but with a little good milk instead of water; boil it up once, and serve it for boiled rabits, scrag or knuckle of veal, or roast mutton. A turnip boiled with the onions makes them milder.

———

# PIES, &c.

## *Eel Pie.*

Cut the the eels in lenghts of two or three inches, season with pepper and salt, and place in the dish, with some bits of butter, and a little water: and cover it with paste.

## *Oatmeal Pudding.*

Pour a quart of boiling milk over a pint of the best *fine* oatmeal; let it soak all night; next day beat two eggs, and mix a little salt; butter a bason that will just hold it; cover it tight with a floured cloth, and boil it an hour and a half. Eat it with cold butter and salt.

When cold, slice and toast it, and eat it as oatcake buttered.

---

### Plain Rice Pudding.

Wash and pick some rice; throw among it some piemento finely pounded, but not much; tie the rice in a cloth, and leave plenty of room for it to swell. Boil it in a quantity of water for an hour or two. When done, eat it with butter and sugar, or milk. Put lemon-peel if you please.

---

### Macaroni Pudding.

Simmer an ounce or two of the pipe sort, in a pint of milk, and a bit of lemon and cinnamon, till tender put it into a dish, with milk, two or three eggs, but only one white, sugar, nutmeg, a spoonful of peach water, and half a glass of wine. Bake with a paste round the edges.

A layer of orange-marmalade, or raspberry jam, in a macaroni pudding, for change, is a great improvement; in which case, omit the almond-water, or ratafia, which you would otherwise flavour it with.

-----

### Pancakes of Rice.

Boil half a pound of rice to a jelly in a small quantity of water; when cold, mix it with a pint of cream, eight eggs, a bit of salt and nutmeg: stir in eight ounces of butter just warmed, and add as

much flour as will make the butter
thick enough.  Fry  in as little lard
or dripping as possible.

---

### Spanish Fritters.

Cut the crumb of  a French roll
into lengths, as thick as your finger,
in what shape  you will.  Soak in
some cream, nutmeg,  sugar, pounded cinnamon, and  an  egg, when
well soaked, fry of  a  nice brown;
and serve  with butter, wine,  and
sugar-sauce.

---

### Lemon Mince Pies.

Squeeze a large  lemon, boil the
outside till  tender  enough  to beat
to a mash,  add  to  it  three  large

apples chopped, and four ounces of suet, half a pound of currants, four ounces of sugar; put the juice of the lemon, and candied fruit, as for other pies. Make a short crust, and fill the pattypans as usual.

---

### Baked Custard.

Boil one pint of cream, half a pint of milk; with mace, cinnamon, and lemon-peel, a little of each. When cold mix the yolks of three eggs; sweeten, and make your cups or paste nearly full. Bake them ten minutes.

---

### Lemon Custards.

Beat the yolks of eight eggs till they are as white as milk : then

put to them a pint of boiling water,
the rinds of two lemons grated and
the juice sweetened to your taste.
Stir it on the fire till thick enou gh ;
then add a large glass of rich wine,
and half a glass of brandy ; give the
whole one scald, and put in cups
to be eaten cold.

---

### Almond Custard.

Blanch and beat four ounces of
almonds fine with a spoonful of
water ; beat a pint of cream with
two spoonful of rose water, and
put them to the yolks of four eggs,
and as much sugar as will make it
pretty sweet ; then add the almonds ; stir it all over a slow fire

till it is of a proper thickness, but don't boil. Pour it into cups.

---

### To stew Onions.

Peel six large onions ; fry gently of a fine brown, but do not blacken them ; then put them into a small stewpan, with a little weak gravy, pepper, and salt ; cover and stew two hours gently. They should be lightly floured at first.

---

## PICKLES, &c.

---

### To pickle red Cabbage.

Slice it into colander, and sprinkle each layer with salt ; let it drain two days, then put it into a jar,

and pour boiling vinegar enough to
cover, and put a few slices of red
beet-root. Observe to choose the
purple red cabbage. Those who
like the flavour of spice will boil it
with the vinegar. Cauliflower cut
in branches, and thrown in after
being salted, will look of a beautiful
red.

---

### Mushroom Ketchup.

Take the largest broad mushrooms, break them into an earthen
pan, strew salt over, and stir them
now and then for three days. Then
let them stand for twelve, till there
is a thick scum over ; strain, and
boil the liquor with Jamaica and
black peppers, mace, ginger, a clove,

or two, and some mustard-seed.
When cold, bottle it, and tie a blad-
der over the cork ; in three months
boil it again with some fresh spice,
and it will then keep a twelve
month.

### Blanc-mange, or Blamange.

Boil two ounces of isinglass in
three half pints of water. half an
hour : strain it to a pint and a half
of cream ; sweeten it, and add some
peach-water, or a few bitter almonds ; let it boil once up, and put
it into what forms you please. If
not to be very stiff, a little less
isinglass will do. Observe to let the
blamange settle before you turn it
into the forms, or the blacks will

remain at the bottom of them, and be on the top of the blamange when taken out of the moulds.

———

*Coffee Cream, much admired.*

Boil a calf's foot in water till it wastes to a pint of jelly, clear of sediment and fat. Make a tea cup of very strong coffee; clear it with a bit of isinglass to be perfectly bright; pour it to the jelly, and add a pint of very good cream, and as much fine sugar as is pleasant; give one boil up, and pour into the dish.

It should be jelly, but not be stiff.

———

## *Ratafia Cream.*

Blanch a quarter of an ounce of bitter almonds, and beat them with a tea spoonful of water in a marble mortar ; then rub with the paste two ounces of lump-sugar, and simmer ten minutes with a tea cup of cream, which add to a quart, more of cream, and having strained, ice it.

---

## *A common Cake.*

Mix three quarters of a pound of flour with half a pound of butter, four ounces of sugar, four eggs, half an ounce of carraways, and a glass of wine. Beat it well, and bake in a quick oven. Fine sugar will do.

## *A good pound Cake.*

Beat a pound of butter to a cream, and mix with it the whites and yolks of eight eggs beaten apart. Have ready warm by the fire, a pound of flour, and the same of sifted sugar, mix them with a few cloves, a little nutmeg and cinnamon, in fine powder together; then by degrees work the dry ingredients into the butter and eggs. When well beaten, add a glass of wine and some carraways. It must be beaten a full hour. Butter a pan, and bake it a full hour in a quick oven.

The above proportions, leaving out four ounces of the butter, and the same of sugar, make a less luscious cake, and to most tastes a more pleasant one.

*To make good Spruce Beer.*

This cheap and wholesome liquor is thus made : take of water sixteen gallons, and boil the half of it; put the water thus boiled, while in full heat, to the reserved cold-part, which should be previously put into a barrel or other vessel : then add **16** pounds of treacle or molasses, with a few table spoonsful of the essence of spruce, stirring the whole well together; and half a pint of yeast, and keep it in a temperate situation, with the bung-hole open for two days, till the fermentation be abated ; then close it up, or bottle it off, and it will be fit to drink in a few days afterwards.

It is a powerful antiscorbutic, and may prove very useful in a long sea voyage.

___

## To make Country or Ginger Beer.

To every gallon of spring water add one ounce of sliced white ginger, one pound of common loaf sugar, and two ounces of lemon juice, or three large table spoonsful; boil it near an hour, and take off the scum, then run it through a hair sieve into a tub, and when cool, (viz. 70°) add yeast in proportion of half a pint to nine gallons; keep it in a temperate situation two days, during, which it may be stirred six or eight times; then put it into a cask, which must be kept full, and the yeast taken off at the bung-hole with spoon. In a fortnight add half a pint of fining (isinglass picked and steeped in beer) to nine gallons, which will, if it has been properly fermented, clear it by ascent. The cask must be kept full, and the rising particles taken off at the bung-hole. When fine, (which may be expected in twenty-four hours) bottle it, cork it well, and in summer it will be ripe, and fit to drink in a fortnight.

**F I N I S.**

# MEASURES AND WEIGHTS

## IN *THE KHWAN NIAMUT*

| | | |
|---|---|---|
| 1 chuttack | 2 ounces | |
| 2 chuttacks | 1/4 pound | |
| 4 chuttacks | 1/2 pound | |
| 8 chuttacks | 1 pound | |
| 16 chuttacks | 2 pounds | |
| 40 rupees | 1 pound | |
| 1 seer | 1 quart | |
| 1 seer | 2 pounds | |
| 40 seers | 1 maund | |
| 1 seer | 16 misqals | 2 pounds |
| 1 tola | 1/5 chuttack | |

# NOTES TO *THE KHWAN NIAMUT*

Pages

title page   **KHWAN NIAMUT:** In Farsi the
meaning is "Table (n.) of Abundance (n.)"
with the suggestion of "A Cuisine of
Riches."

Nawab: According to *A Handbook for Travellers in India, Burma and Ceylon*, "Nawab
(Arabic) means literally 'deputies' being
the plural of na'ib, 'a deputy.' It is now a
title of Governors and other high officials."

Buhadur: *A Handbook for Travellers in India,
Burma and Ceylon* defines this as a Persian
honorific, meaning brave or chivalric, used
as a title of honor among Muhammadans.

17   Zeerah: cumin.

19   Khichree: scrambled. Mary S. Atwood, in *A
Taste of India*, describes "Kitchri" as a
dish made of rice and dhal (lentils) and
adds that "it originated as an invalid
dish and now there are ever so many
variations."

Biryan: an elaborate pulao, where rice is
layered with spiced meats and vegetables.
Atwood defines "Biryani—a rich dish con-

sisting of layers of partially cooked rice and curried meat cooked together until done, using a fire beneath and hot charcoal on the lid; a Moglai dish."

22 Quorema: a rich braised curry, usually containing yogurt.
   Duhee (Tyre): "Dahi": sour curd, or buttermilk, yogurt.

28 Puneer: fresh cheese similar to cottage cheese.

32 Khaginah: an omelette.

36 Urug-i-Nuanea: vinegar.

37 Kaghuzee: lemons.

39 Musoor: pink or salmon lentils.

41 Belen, Belun: a roller or rolling pin.

44 Pooree: fried "balloon" breads.

54 depurated: purified.

59 negus: type of beverage, after Col. Francis Negus (died 1732), made of wine, hot water, sugar, nutmeg, and lemon juice.

69 forth: i.e., froth.

85 ratafia: liqueur flavored with bitter almond.

95 treacle: molasses, sometimes specifically the molasses which drains from the sugar-refining molds.